1 Peter

1 Peter

Authentic
LIFESTYLE

First published in 2003 by Authentic Lifestyle

09 08 07 06 05 04 03   7 6 5 4 3 2 1

Authentic Lifestyle is an imprint of Authentic Media,
P.O. Box 300, Carlisle, Cumbria, CA3 0QS, UK
and
P.O. Box 1047, Waynesboro, GA 30830–2047, USA

Website: www.paternoster-publishing.com

British Library Cataloguing in Publication Data
A catalogue record for this book is available from the British Library

ISBN 1-85078-527-9

Cover Design by Diane Bainbridge
Typeset by WestKey Ltd, Falmouth, Cornwall
Printed in Great Britain by Bell & Bain Ltd, Glasgow

Contents

For Tom and Katie, Luke, Alex and Tom
for the different ways in whih you
have helped me with the Study Guides

Your Faith - of Greater Worth Than Gold

Key Truth: Jesus has shown us the pattern of suffering first, glory later. Therefore we can endure trials now because our eyes are fixed on our future hope.

1. God's Elect - Strangers in the World (1:1-2)

Peter doesn't address his letter to a single church, but to 'the Church scattered throughout the world', to those who are not at home in the world as it now is. He uses the word 'diaspora' to refer to this **chosen** people, a word that is used to refer to 'exile' in the Greek translation of the Hebrew Scriptures.[1] The Church is chosen by the Living God but still living in 'exile' until the appearing of Jesus the Messiah. We will see that everything that Peter writes can only be properly understood in the light of the Hebrew Scriptures, to which he constantly refers throughout the letter.

Why did Peter write this letter? He tells us in chapter 5:12. He wants to encourage the 'chosen exiles' to **stand fast** in the true grace of God.

As exiles and pilgrims in the world we are under the constant temptation to blend in with the world. We are different because we belong to the Living God in a world that lies under the influence of the devil. **Standing fast** in the favour of the True God sets us in contrast to the rest of the world, and will certainly bring us persecution and suffering. The apostle Peter wrote this letter to strengthen and encourage the Church throughout the world to endure these sufferings with confidence in the glories that will come when Jesus the Messiah returns.

The encouragement begins straight away. Peter calls the Church 'elect' to give us security when the world rejects us. He reminds us that

---

[1] See Deuteronomy 28:25; 30:4; Nehemiah 1:9.

the whole Trinity works for the Church. The Father knew the Church long ago, the Holy Spirit is at work to sanctify it, and through the blood of Jesus we are obedient. We stand, not by any of our own merits but simply through the work of the Trinity. For these immovable reasons we know that the world can never finally overcome the Church.

2. New Birth to a Resurrection Hope (1:3–5)

After such a sobering introduction about being strange exiles in the world, we might imagine that Peter would need some cheering up, but he launches into praise – 'Praise be to the God and Father of our Lord Jesus Christ!' What can make Peter so thankful when as a Christian he faces a life of suffering?

Peter has his eyes fixed on the future. Once we see what the future holds for the Church through Jesus the Messiah then we can even rejoice in our present sufferings. Stoical endurance is not enough to carry us through suffering with thankfulness: we need the glorious hope of our resurrection future.

We have a new birth. Our first birth promised us death, but this new birth promises resurrection. Our hope is **living** not dying; **permanent** not fading. It is guaranteed by the resurrection of Jesus Christ.

We have seen in Jesus how resurrection came **after** His own suffering and death, therefore we know that since we are in Him we will receive the same. Our inheritance in Christ is everlasting, not like the temporary rewards that this passing age can give us. The whole universe will be renewed when Christ returns and we will inherit it all with Him. Nothing can take this away from us. Jesus Christ is in heaven beyond all the powers of evil and decay, keeping the resurrection future safe until He returns. Our inheritance is for the future, but it is a rock-solid certain hope that can sustain us through suffering **now**.

We are shielded by God's power in our present lives as we trust Him to deliver all that is safely waiting for us in Jesus Christ. When He is revealed on the final day, then our salvation will be given to us. **Then** we will receive all the joy, health, prosperity, peace and comfort of the New Creation. It is all 'ready to be revealed' – nothing more needs to be done. Whatever happens to us now, this inheritance cannot be harmed in any way.

Meditating on all this lies at the very centre of Peter's message for the Church. We can only endure to the end if we live with our eyes fixed on the end.

3. Suffering Proves Faith (1:6-7)

It is this great and living hope that makes us 'greatly rejoice'. It is impossible to spend too much time thinking about the New Creation hope that is guaranteed to us in Jesus. The more we learn about it from Scripture the more thrilled with it we become.

This great rejoicing happens even though right now, 'for a little while', we have to 'suffer grief in all kinds of trials'.

But why? Why do we have to suffer grief for a little while?

Peter explains. It is only in our sufferings that the reality of our faith is displayed. It is only in our trials that our trust in Jesus Christ is shown to be authentic. In the hardest times, when all that is false and trivial is stripped away, only our faith in Jesus Christ can survive. We may well lose everything else, including our earthly riches. However, if we understand the real worth of this trust in Jesus, then we can deal with the loss of everything else.

Suffering makes us see the true value of things. What do we really need for life and eternity? What is truly essential? Suffering is able to refine us, showing us that trusting Jesus is infinitely more valuable than everything else we have. It has been said that 'trials are God's multi-gym for faith muscles.'

We must remember that suffering is transformed into this amazing benefit only by the almighty power of the Living God. Without trust in Jesus, suffering may produce nothing but bitterness and sorrow.

For the Church, the final outcome of this temporary suffering is the praise and glory and honour of Jesus Christ. When He is revealed, then the fact that His people trusted Him through it all will show just how wonderful and praiseworthy He is. It will be an eternal testimony to His glory. A person who can command trust through such 'fiery trials' (4:12) is a person worthy of honour!

4. Love and Joy From Proven Faith (1:8-9)

Peter continues the thought. Jesus Christ can sustain our trust through every trial, and we keep loving Him even though we cannot see Him. That is what faith is all about – trusting when we cannot see. We know all about Jesus Christ and we have seen how suffering and glory worked in His life, so we depend on Him for our own life.

As we trust Him we are filled with 'an inexpressible and glorious joy'. Why? Because we are receiving the very thing we trust Him for – the salvation of our souls. If we are trusting Jesus to take away all our trials and sufferings in **this** life, then we will be filled with nothing but an inexpressible and terrible **disappointment**. He has promised us sufferings **now** and glory **later**. However, if we see that our salvation is the inheritance of the future when He is revealed, then we are filled with this unspeakable joy. Suffering actually has a purpose for the person who trusts Jesus: focussing our hearts and minds on our indestructible inheritance.

5. Looking Forward to the Glories After Suffering (1:10–12)

The Old Testament Church is a great encouragement for us to keep putting our faith in the Messiah. These early believers trusted that the Messiah would be glorified after His sufferings. The Holy Spirit gave them many prophecies of the Messiah's sufferings and glory, and they studied these Scriptures intently with the greatest care as they kept on trusting in Him. The Holy Spirit told them that through these predictions they would serve the later Church.

The Old Testament saints trusted that the Messiah's glories would **follow** His sufferings – and they were completely vindicated in that trust. They longed to know how and when it would all happen... but they trusted that it **would** all happen just as predicted. Well, we have seen just how right they were to trust in those prophecies because we have read the eyewitness accounts of the sufferings and glory of the Messiah. Therefore, we should have an even greater confidence in the pattern of glory **following** suffering. They have served us through their patient trust.

Jesus summarised the teaching of the Hebrew Scriptures in just this way – see Luke 24:13 & 24:44. The Hebrew Scriptures are full of these prophecies of suffering for the Messiah **first** followed by **later** glory. We see this in Genesis 3:15, when the Serpent would **first** bruise the heel of the Seed, even though **afterwards** He would crush the Serpent's head. In Genesis 22 we see Abraham predict that the Lamb of God would be **first** sacrificed on Mount Moriah **then** be resurrected. In Psalm 2 we see that **first** the nations plot against the LORD and His Messiah, but that **in the end** the Son rules over all. Psalm 22 predicted the sufferings of the Messiah on the Cross, but also His **later** glory. In Zechariah 12:10–13:1 the prophet predicted that salvation from sin would come only **after** the LORD had been pierced. There are hundreds of examples of the Holy Spirit sustaining the Old Testament saints with predictions of the suffering and glory of Jesus the Messiah.

The purpose of these predictions was to show how the pattern of **'suffering now, glory later'** is not a foolish hope. The Old Testament saints trusted that Jesus Christ would only be glorified **after** suffering, and they were right. Even the angels would love to investigate the great truths of the Messiah's sufferings and glory. Yet, we have been given these deep mysteries not so that we can be superior to angels, but so that we can live fruitful lives to Christ's honour and glory.

If we do not understand that suffering is for **now** and glory for **later**, we will turn away from Jesus when things get tough. The Holy Spirit was sent from heaven to tell us this gospel. We need to receive it and trust it as the most precious truth there has ever been.

Further Questions ...

1. What is an apostle (verse 1)? See passages such as Mark 3:14; 1 Corinthians 9:1–2; 15:7–9; Galatians 1:1.

2. What does it mean to be God's elect (verse 1)? See passages such as Psalm 106:4–5; Isaiah 42:1–4; Luke 9:35; Ephesians 1:3–14.

3. What is our inheritance? See passages such as Isaiah 65:17–25; Romans 8:18–21.

Daily Readings ...

Day 1:	1 Peter 1:1–12
Day 2:	James chapter 1
Day 3:	Hebrews chapter 11
Day 4:	Isaiah chapter 53
Day 5:	Luke chapter 2
Day 6:	Romans chapter 8
Day 7:	Revelation chapter 21

BIBLE STUDY 1

1 Peter 1:1–9

1. How do we define 'the world', verse 1? What does it mean practically to be 'strangers' in it?

2. What does verse 2 tell us about how our salvation came about? How is this an encouragement especially during times of persecution? (See Romans 8:31)

3. How was our 'living hope' achieved? How does this help us to understand what it is? See 1 Corinthians 15:20–26.

4. Compare the treasures of verse 4 and verse 7. Think, too, about what Jesus teaches about treasure in Matthew 6:19–20. How can we make sure that our hearts are set on our heavenly inheritance? What practical steps can we take to ensure that what we hope for in Jesus is more important than what we own or want to own?

5. How is Peter teaching us to look on trials and difficult times, verses 6–7?

6. What does this passage tell us to rejoice in? Are we ever to rejoice about suffering itself? How can we possibly rejoice?

7. How can we love Jesus if we've never seen Him, verses 8–9? What does this teach us about love? (See also John 14:15)

Born Again - Through the
Word of God

Key Truth: As Christians, all our blessings and our identity is found in Jesus. We depend on Him and desire the Bible for spiritual nourishment.

1. Minds Set for Action (1:13-16)

Having filled our minds with great excitement and wonder at the gospel of Christ's sufferings and glory, Peter tells us to get all this truth organised for **action**. There are 6 commands from 1:13-2:3 – prepare, do not conform, be holy, live in fear, love, desire the word.

We prepare our minds in advance. It's too late in the heat of the moment when the temptation to compromise and remain anonymous feels overwhelming. However, the first action for which Peter says our minds must be ready is a kind of inaction. We must be self-controlled, which is defined as NOT conforming to the evil desires we used to have. We will never be able to live differently unless we think differently. Peter has shown us the amazing truths that must fill our minds to make us ready to turn away from evil desires. In Matthew 6:21 Jesus said 'where your treasure is, there your heart will be also.' Our desires show what we really want, what we most value. Once we valued evil desires, and although we still have these, we now value Jesus and His imperishable inheritance above all else. Therefore we want to be holy in all we do.

What does 'holy' mean? Verse 14 defines it for us. To be holy is to be like Christ. In Leviticus 11:44–45 we see that because the LORD freed the Israelites from Egyptian slavery, so they were to be like Him. If we have been freed from empty lives of ignorance, we want to be like our Rescuer.

2. Precious Before the World Began (1:17–21)

With our heavenly Father we find justice. He judges all things impartially and accurately. Therefore, knowing that His eye is upon us and that His assessment of us is all that matters, we are able to cope with the injustice we will experience because of the gospel. **Now** we will have to put up with constant injustice, false accusations, ridicule and hatred. With our 'future vision' we can remain faithful through all this. We don't seek revenge or try to establish our own kind of justice, whether through the courts or our own schemes. If we are living as strangers **waiting** with reverent fear for the Day of Judgement, then we can avoid being embroiled in inappropriate demands for earthly justice right now. It is so easy to be drawn into saying 'sure I will enjoy justice from God one day, but actually I **demand** my rights and my justice **right now**!' It is a powerful gospel witness when we show that being vindicated by the Living God is more important to us than being vindicated by humanity.

We can only invest so completely and confidently in Jesus when we realise what a firm investment He is. Thieves can steal gold and the most cherished human traditions always become dated. However, Jesus is more valuable than everything in the universe, because His Father chose Him before the universe began, verse 20. When we trust Jesus we are investing with the Living God. We can make the costly choices now only if we grasp the value of Jesus. We will never put our job, money, house, friends, family or future at risk for Him unless we see that He far out-weighs all of these things.

3. Growing, not Perishing (1:22–2:3)

'Love one another deeply from the heart' (1:22). Those are words that everybody in the world seems to agree with – yet for Peter they are not abstract words of utopian idealism, but words of practical necessity – a basic statement of church life. Once we follow Jesus into costly suffering, it is the love and support of the Christian community that makes it possible or bearable.

As Christians, we have purified ourselves by obeying the truth – 1:22. We have been born again, not according to the corrupt, sinful, perishable human nature that we were first born with... but according to the pure, incorruptible nature of Jesus Christ Himself. He is the Seed who was promised from the very beginning of the Bible. There is a wonderful harmony in that the 'Word of God' is a single phrase that covers both the Second Person of the Trinity, Jesus Christ, and also the Bible. Both are called 'the Word of God' in the Bible, because there is a such a deep unity between them. The purpose of the Bible is to make us trust in Jesus. He is the central character of the whole Bible, the One that Moses and the Prophets wrote about, (John 1:45). It is as the Bible (the word of God) is preached that people meet Jesus (the Word of God). We have been re-born into the new humanity of the Messiah, and while the old nature, verse 24, is fixed on the here and now, our new nature is born through the Word of God that lasts forever.

Sincere love is practical and genuine. Mere sentiments don't answer real needs. Because the word of the LORD has shown us the true value of everything, we can show love from the heart, not **just** from the mouth or the wallet. So, 2:1, we get rid of all malice towards each other, and deceit – the very opposite of sincere love. Our energy needs to be focussed on bringing people to Jesus, so we can't afford to aggravate each other. But if our values are based merely on human glory, our motives will always be mixed with malice, deceit, hypocrisy, envy and slander. Sincere love for each other shows how we have been freed from fading glory.

Peter's great encouragement to us is to reflect on the word of God that both began our Christian life (1:23) and sustains us, making us grow (2:2). As we develop cravings for the constant nourishment of the word of God, the Bible, so we will experience spiritual growth – which has little to do with some vague 'inner serenity' and everything to do with **practical love** for the Christian family. The world sees spirituality in strange, other-worldly feelings, but Jesus has shown us that true spirituality is shown in following Him into the rough and tumble of self-sacrifice and practical love.

If we wish to be true to our new birth in Christ, we must crave the one thing that will cause us to spiritually grow.

Cravings tell us a great deal about a person. What do we crave? What gives us withdrawal symptoms when we miss it for too long? What do we turn to for refreshment when we are depleted? Here the apostle Peter tells us to crave the word of God just like a newborn baby craves milk. The new-born baby cries until it gets its milk. It has an instinct for pure nourishing milk because that milk is life – it will cause it to grow up and fend off disease.

Why? Why is the word of God something that we must develop an obsessive fixation for, something that we must become irresistibly addicted to? As we immerse ourselves in the Bible we are getting spiritual nourishment. As we give ourselves to the word of God, we are not taking up some kind of intellectual hobby. We are having our hearts and minds shaped by the heart and mind of the Living God.

Peter reminds us in 1:24 of the great words of Isaiah 40. The only real comfort in life and death is the word of the LORD, because it belongs to eternal life. It brings us what is true and final and nourishing. We can only invest in the future as we invest in the gospel of Jesus Christ.

4. A Spiritual Temple (2:4–8)

Peter gives us the image of a temple being built. Jesus is the Living Stone, the Foundation Stone, the Stone that the temple depends upon. He is chosen by God but rejected by humanity.

It is important that Peter tells us this, because Christians are also chosen by God but rejected by humanity. We share the glory of Jesus, but we **also** share His rejection and suffering. Everybody wants the glory and power of the resurrection after death (and how many cults love to shout about that!), but the path to the resurrection is through the Cross. There can be no avoiding this.

So, as stones from the Living Stone, we are being built, by the Holy Spirit, into a temple – but we are not just the stones of this temple, we are also its priests, verse 5.

The Hebrew Scriptures prepare us well to understand the job of a priest. A priest stands between the LORD God and humanity. This is exactly what Christians do. We stand between the LORD God and humanity, passing on God's gospel to the world, and bringing people to Jesus. 2 Corinthians 5:20 – God makes His appeal to the world through us. Notice that **every** stone is part of this priesthood. It is not as if only **some** Christians are priestly – **every** stone has this job.

We are a **holy** priesthood. By this Peter means something quite specific. In chapter 1 verses 14–15 he defines what he means. We are holy in that we no longer live as we used to live following those evil desires. If we have blended in with non-Christians then we are not advocating our Holy God on His behalf. But, on the other hand, if we cut ourselves off from the world, we also fail as priests. An unbiblical separation from life in the world can never be Biblical holiness. Living on an island (either literally or metaphorically) with our fellow Christians may make us **feel** wonderfully in harmony with the creation and each other, but it is a betrayal of our identity in Jesus.

Peter quotes from Isaiah 28:16 – a prophecy about the Messiah as the foundation stone of the people of God. The context of this quotation is crucial. Isaiah was speaking to the nation of Judah. The nation had entered into a pact with Egypt to protect them from invasion. Isaiah is telling them not to trust in Egypt but to trust in the LORD, the only One who will not disappoint them. Throughout the Bible Egypt symbolises the pagan world with all its self-confidence and pride. But, to avoid the suffering that is coming to Judah, Judah trusts in Egypt.

This is why Peter chooses this quotation. The great temptation for his readers was to make peace with the world to avoid the persecution they faced. This might indeed buy some temporary relief from suffering – but it will end in (verses 7–8) stumbling, falling and shame.

The faithful Christian trusts in Jesus even when it brings temporary suffering – because in the end there will be no shame or stumbling for the person who trusts in the Messiah. Jesus divides humanity into those who trust in Him, and those who reject Him. Those who reject Him cannot escape Him – they are destined to stumble over Him and fall.

5. A People Belonging to God (2:9–10)

In trusting Jesus our lives are united to Him. He is chosen, so we are too. He is the royal priest, so we are too. He is holy, so we are too. He is rejected, so we get rejected too. Everything that we are comes from Jesus Christ. Given how precious He is, we can be confident, even though we stand out so starkly from the world that rejects Jesus.

Peter is drawing from the evangelistic instructions of the Old Testament, from both Exodus and Isaiah. His description of the Church here in 2:9 is from Exodus 19:5–6. Peter also notes how Isaiah challenged the Church in **his** day to declare the praises of the Messiah – Isaiah 42:6, 43:20–1, 49:6.

We do not declare His praises in the abstract – simply saying 'praise Jesus' over and over again. Such words alone don't mean anything to the rest of humanity. Rather we praise Him by explaining all that He has done for us, for calling us out of the unbelief and evil desires we used to follow – into His marvellous light.

This is why our lives have to be so different from the pagans. If they are not, then no-one will see what the marvellous light is that we have been called into. A dim glimmer is not so marvellous.

The Christian who does not declare these praises to others hasn't appreciated what Peter tells us in verse 10. The phrase 'not a people' comes from Hosea 1:10 & 2:23. The LORD told Hosea to marry Gomer, a prostitute. This was to show that although His people were wicked and faithless, yet He would woo them back. Read Hosea 3:1–3. We might think it impossible for Hosea to continue to love his wife and restore her to himself, yet Jesus has loved us and restored us from even worse and much more dangerous adultery – spiritual adultery. These are the praises we must declare to the world that remains in spiritual prostitution.

Once we were nobodies – living pointless lives under the anger of God heading for destruction. But now we are the people who belong to the LORD God of Israel. Grasping what we were apart from Christ makes 9a more wonderful and makes us ready to do 9b.

Further Questions ...

1. When people talk about 'priests' in general culture they tend to think about an elite group of church officials rather than every Christian believer. How can a deeper understanding of 'priesthood' change this? See Exodus 19:3–6; Romans 15:15–16; Hebrews 10:11–14.

2. One of the great cultural pressures from the world today is to remain agnostic about life after death or eternal judgement. What is the fate of those who do not believe in Jesus, 2:8? Matthew 25:41. How can we faithfully speak these truths when we will face such hostility for doing so?

3. 'Born again' has become a buzz phrase for fresh starts. On the other hand 'born-again Christians' are sometimes portrayed as a weird and fanatical kind of Christian. Look at 1:23 and passages such as John 3:1–15, Titus 3:4–7, 1 John 5:1–5. Exactly how are we born again?

Daily Readings ...

Day 1:   1 Peter 1:13–2:10

Day 2:   Deuteronomy 10:12–11:32

Day 3:   Isaiah chapter 28

Day 4:   Isaiah chapter 40

Day 5:   Leviticus chapter 19

Day 6:   Psalm 118

Day 7:   Ephesians chapter 1

BIBLE STUDY 2

1 Peter 1:22–2:10

1. How does Peter say we have purified ourselves? (see John 17:17)
   Compare verse 22 with 2:1. What is strange about the command of
   2:1 if we have already done 1:22? What do we learn about ourselves?

2. Who is the 'imperishable Seed' (verse 23)? See Galatians 3:16 which
   explains Genesis 12:7, and Genesis 3:15.

3. Remembering verses 22–25 of chapter 1, what is the 'spiritual milk' to
   which Peter refers, 2:2? What is our motivation for growing, 2:3?

4. In 2:4–5 we are living stones joined to The Living Stone, Jesus. How
   can **we** be encouraged by the Father's view of Jesus?

5. What is the 'spiritual house' in 2:5? Who lives in it (see Hebrews 3:6)?
   Who are the priests, 2:5?

6. What are the sacrifices offered in this temple by these priests? What
   does this mean for us? (see Hebrews 13:16, Psalm 51:17)

7. Can anyone escape Jesus, verses 6–8? What are the two possible
   reactions to Him?

8. What are the great privileges of being a Christian, verse 9? Looking at
   2:4, why do we have these privileges?

9. What are we called to do, 2:9? What does this mean? How does
   knowing verse 10 inspire us to do verse 9?

Christ Suffered - Leaving an Example

Key Truth: We will stand out and be rejected by the world because of our Christ-like behaviour in all areas of our lives.

1. Such Good Lives (2:11-12)

We can only fulfil our priestly duties to declare the praises of Christ if we see ourselves as aliens and strangers in the world, verse 11. We are citizens of the New Creation, the new order that will be unveiled at the appearing of Jesus Christ. We have no ultimate stake in this passing age. If we are not fully convinced of this we will never declare the praises of Christ with the faithful confidence that we should. If we are trying to build our future here and now we will try to stay out of the line of fire and appear as if we were normal citizens of this present darkness. **But** the very things that the pagan thinks of as harmless and enjoyable are actually spiritual suicide. They make war on our souls, verse 11. Because the Christian not only knows this but also lives and declares it, we are inevitably seen as aliens and strangers. We just don't fit in with the pattern of pagan life. We are disruptive.

But, Peter doesn't want us to be oddballs simply for the fun of it. It is a key part of our priestly duties – verse 12. Our lives must be like he has described so that the pagans may see how we live, become Christians and glorify God on the day that He comes to visit. Holy living is not a selfish quest for personal purity, but an outward looking mission to the glory of the Living God.

God the Father has made us into a holy nation whose behaviour appears so strange to the pagans who meet us. Sometimes we might think it is best to be exactly like non-Christians in order to be 'authentic witnesses', but such thinking can be very dangerous. Our message is **not**:

'see how we are exactly like you… see how little difference the divine Messiah has made to our lives'!

Notice that Peter is well aware that the pagans will accuse us of doing wrong. Today, telling others that they **have** to trust only in Jesus to avoid the terrible fate of Judgement Day is perceived to be deeply offensive. It flies in the face of the most sacred canons of post-modern society. The modern world treats all 'religions' (including Christianity) as the same. All are reduced to equally valuable quests for 'spirituality'. If we testify that only the Way of Jesus is true, our witness seems totally unacceptable. But, we have no choice. Our great passion is the glory of God – and as Peter tells us, the One True God is glorified when people become Christians.

We are priests addicted to the glory of God. Even though we stick out like a sore thumb, even though we face the rejection of our culture and our pagan friends, yet we cannot help declaring the praises of Him who called us out of darkness into His wonderful light.

2. Submission and Freedom (2:13–17)

Submission is the way we live out the good life of verse 12. Submission is the key word for 2:13; 2:18 and 3:1. It is a word that strikes terror into the self-assertiveness of our sinful desires.

Peter picks the issue of submission to civil authorities as the first test of our 'good deeds'. Why? In his day the governing authority was the Roman Empire, a fascist state with one of the most terrible human rights records in history. Peter definitely wasn't thinking of an easy-to-follow liberal democracy! Yet, under such a godless and pagan regime as the Roman Empire, a regime that would murder countless thousands of Christians, the gospel leads us to **submission** – 'for the LORD's sake'. Our love of Christ outweighs our concern for our own rights and privileges. The civil authorities are supposed to maintain law and order, so the Church will be a model of civil obedience.

Shouldn't our passion for justice and truth and freedom lead us to rebellion and revolution? Shouldn't we try to overthrow the pagan systems of government in order to enforce the way of Jesus? No, the truly revolutionary action is to be a faithful witness to Jesus Christ to the people who live in our street or block of flats. Have we presented Jesus to the people we work with, the parents of our children's friends, our local shopkeepers or the other members of our gym? Is our local church a haven of justice, truth, freedom and compassion? Do we love the brothers and sisters in our local church in obvious and practical ways?

People **will** accuse us of doing wrong (verse 12), but because we submit to the state's law and order, they will have nothing against us (verse

15). It goes without saying, of course, that the Church will never submit to any authority that commands us to turn against Christ.

The non-Christian defines 'freedom' as 'freedom to do exactly what I want' even though they never have true freedom because of the tyranny of sin – chapter 4:2–4. The Church experiences the true freedom of life in Christ, but we use our **freedom** for the **service** of God, not the service of our sinful desires.

Showing proper respect for everyone, verse 17, reveals the glory of the gospel. We are not intimidated or controlled by worldly evaluations. We love the Church, and because we fear God we honour the king without fearing him.

3. Suffering at Work for Christ (2:18–20)

From the macro, Peter zooms in to the workplace. The employer/ employee parallel seems to capture the issues here. The fundamental issues in an ancient slave's life are the same ones that face us in the modern 'rat race' – diligence, submission, hard work and relationship tensions. How many of us are tied into jobs that are not what we want? We shouldn't exaggerate the theoretical freedoms of the modern age, but face up to the day-to-day demands of the workplace.

The Church's mission is not to fight for better treatment in the workplace, but to submit to the boss with all respect, even when the boss is harsh and unjust. This must all be understood under the heading of suffering with Christ with our eyes fixed on later glory. The fact that the Church suffers such injustice is part of our priestly duties, showing to the world that we are more conscious of the Living God than our own cause. We know that suffering is the will of God for us – 1:6–7 – therefore we can endure injustice. Suffering injustice with our eyes on the appearing of Jesus is radically different and incomprehensible to the pagan world. It shows that we really do believe the gospel of Jesus.

The one thing we must avoid at all costs is suffering for doing **wrong**. If our employers punish us for meddling, time-wasting or dishonesty then we undermine our gospel witness. We are faithful to Christ only when we suffer for doing **good**. All suffering is not good – only gospel driven suffering is a presentation of Christ.

4. Christ's Example (2:21–25)

Submission to the state and employers, even when facing harsh injustice, may not seem possible or desirable. Won't this just come across as weak and pathetic? Peter directs our attention to Jesus Himself as the example of what this looks like in practice.

Verse 21 begins by reminding us that we were called to suffer injustice for doing good. When we think about what the Father is 'calling' us to do, we tend to put the emphasis on things like 'what career am I being **called** into?'. However, Peter shakes us out of our comfort. If we are genuinely asking what the Father is calling us to do, we can be sure that He is calling us to **suffer injustice for the gospel**. What career we do is unimportant compared to whether we faithfully suffer injustice for the gospel.

It is always good to review our priorities – not as we **think** they should be, but as they **really** are in our daily living. What dominates our conversations with our fellow Christians? What do we spend the most time talking about or worrying about? Sometimes we might say things like 'I know that in the light of eternity it doesn't really matter, but…', followed by what may well be a true picture of what really fills our hearts and minds in practice.

Jesus did not set us an example of how to discover the right career, but He showed us how to suffer in a Godly way so that we would 'follow in His steps', verse 21.

Jesus was certainly not inferior or weak compared to those who insulted and murdered Him. He had legions of angels at His disposal and justice on His side. He had the right to retaliate, to call retribution down on His accusers. But He didn't do any of this. Isaiah (53:9) had prophesied how Jesus would endure harsh injustice with sinless, silent patience.

How could Jesus do this? It is not a hidden secret. Jesus kept His mind fixed on the future. Verse 23 – He entrusted Himself to the just judgements of His Father. It did not matter to Jesus how humans judged Him if He was approved by His Father. He knew that He was carrying out His Father's will and that meant more to Him than anything else. That is our example. If the Father will judge justly we can live with injustice now. This liberates us from the need to right wrongs in our own strength. Such actions simply show that we are not entrusting ourselves to the Father.

Verse 24 shows us how we can be confident in this. The Cross shows that the Living God cares about injustice. Through the Cross we are **right** before God, so we don't have to prove we are right before men. True justice is established through the injustice inflicted on Jesus. We cannot look at the Cross and demand our rights! We **deserve** hell, yet we've been forgiven. We were lost and under the power of sinful desires but Jesus doesn't make war on our souls (as sin does in 2:11); He cares for our souls, (2:25). He looks after our best eternal interests. If He has shown us the way to submit, we are in no position to question His example. We owe everything to Him.

5. Evangelism in Marriage (3:1–3:7)

Finally Peter brings us to marriage to see how we must submit to the world. Our priestly evangelistic duties go on in marriage just as they do in politics and work.

Submission becomes an issue only when there is disagreement. After the Fall (see Genesis 3:16 and 4:19), neither husband or wife want to submit to each other. **Therefore** this is a great opportunity to display the gospel. The Christian has learned submission in every area of life from the example of Jesus Christ. Submission is the way of evangelism in politics and work, so it is also the way in marriage – 3:1. It is the purity and fear (**of God** – see 2:17) of the wife that will draw the unbelieving husband to Christ. Her fear of the Living God liberates her from the fears of her husband. She can be both submissive and free from intimidation, because her identity is not found in her husband but in Jesus Christ. The wife will be beautiful to her husband, not by following the shallow 'beauty myths' of the world, but through the inner, unfading beauty of a gentle and quiet spirit.

This view must not be caricatured. Peter gives us Sarah as the model wife in all this, and he refers us specifically to Genesis 18 for instruction. When Sarah refers to Abraham as her master, she is laughing to herself at the thought of old Abraham being able to give her the pleasure of procreation any more. Her respect for Abraham is affectionate and full of good humour.

However, Peter is trying to address the situation of a wife married to a non-Christian husband. That is why he adds the end of verse 6. The Christian wife follows Sarah when she does what is right and is not intimidated by any fear. Her husband may try to intimidate her in all kinds of ways, but because she fears the Living God, she can respect her husband and be free from fear.

When Peter turns to husbands he continues the same track. If the husband is going to present the gospel to his wife, he must not be at all domineering. Husbands are nearly always physically stronger than their wives, but the husband must never use this strength against his wife. Domestic violence is very common, but the Christian husband must never give way to it. It should never be covered over with mere remorse. Life is a gracious gift. It is not deserved, but generously given by the Father. The husband and wife are **equal** heirs together of this gift. This gracious equality must mark a husband's relationship with his wife.

The consequence of failing to live life as equal heirs of the gracious gift is the hindering of prayer. Presumably the Father will not hear the prayers of those who deny grace in their marriage – Psalm 66:18. Throughout the epistle we learn that we cannot separate our relationship with Christ from any part of our lives.

Further Questions ...

1. What is the war of the soul mentioned in 2:11? See passages such as Romans 7:21–25; Galatians 5:16–26.

2. Compare Acts 4:18–20 with 1 Peter 2:13. Has Peter changed his mind? When is it right to submit to human authorities and when not?

3. Why does Peter tell wives to be subject to husbands and not the other way round? See Genesis 2:18–25, 3:16; Ephesians 5:21–33.

Daily Readings ...

Day 1:	1 Peter 2:11–3:7
Day 2:	Romans chapter 13
Day 3:	Isaiah chapter 53
Day 4:	Matthew chapter 26
Day 5:	Genesis chapter 2
Day 6:	Ephesians chapter 5
Day 7:	Ephesians chapter 6

BIBLE STUDY 3

1 Peter 2:18-25

1. Why does God expect us to suffer injustice and not fight against it, verse 19?

2. What does Peter mean by saying the words, 'conscious of God', see 1 Corinthians 4: 5 and Romans 12:19? What keeps us from hitting out at our accusers?

3. What might we be tempted to do under the circumstances of unjust suffering, verse 20? What are we to do instead, and why? (verses 21–23)

4. What thoughts encouraged Jesus as He was enduring the most terrible suffering the world has ever known? (verses 23–24; also Isaiah 53:7–12; and Christ's thoughts on the Cross, shown to us in Psalm 22:16–22) How can we follow His example in suffering?

5. We might sometimes be tempted to think that the Lord doesn't care about injustice if we are to endure it. How do verses 23–24 show the extent of how He cares?

6. We often want to fit in and be accepted by our friends and colleagues and be the same as them. But how do verses 24 and 25 show us the difference in the way God looks on a Christian in comparison to a non-Christian? (See also Psalm 34:15, 2 Corinthians 5:17.) In what ways can we encourage each other when we are tempted to keep quiet about our faith for this reason?

7. How often do we suffer **for the gospel** in our workplace or amongst unbelieving friends? Do others know why we are taking a stand or behaving differently? Think of opportunities we may have to explain our reasons and pray that we would be courageous in doing these over the coming weeks.

Suffering for What is Right – Armed With Christ's Attitude

Key Truth: With Jesus as our example, we do not fear what people think but serve the Lord, suffering for the good that we do.

1. Repay Evil With Blessing (3:8–12)

The way the Christian church lives as a family is one of the most powerful testimonies to the gospel – whether for good or bad. If we **fight** with each other we are telling the world that Jesus is not the answer to their problems. Yet, if we **love** one another with sympathy, compassion and humility, even when we have lots of reasons to disagree, then it is clear that Jesus is the Prince of Peace.

Does the **life** of our local church agree with what we **say** about Jesus our Saviour and Lord?

When we suffer evil then we are tested. What really motivates us? What governs our behaviour?

Peter reminds us of Psalm 34 when David had to deal with evil against him. When David went to Gath he listened to what the Philistines were saying against him (1 Samuel 21:10–15) and he became very frightened. In this state of fear he behaved like a madman and could offer nothing of any use to Achish the king of the Philistines.[1]

---

[1] Although he is called Achish, every king of the Philistines also seemed to have the honorary title of 'Abimelech' meaning 'father of the king' (like the title 'Pharoah' for the Egyptians). This title is used at the beginning of Psalm 34. See Genesis 20 and 26. Sometimes people have confused this with the incident about David visiting Ahimelech at the shrine at Nob in 1 Samuel

In Psalm 34 David teaches us the key lesson from this incident. When David had faced wild animals as a shepherd boy and when he had faced Goliath in 1 Samuel 17, he had trusted in the LORD and been free of fear. When David gave into the fear of men, then he had only madness to give the Philistines for their insults – evil for evil. If he had remembered that his LORD Messiah is always listening to those who trust Him, always ready to support them in troubled times, then he would have been able to give gospel blessings to the Philistines.

2. Set Apart Christ as Lord (3:13–16)

Peter begins by pointing out the obvious – verse 13. If we are people of love, compassion and humility, we are not going to attract the kind of hatred and aggravation that hateful, cruel and arrogant people do. Nevertheless, verses 14–22, suffering for doing good is a feature of following Jesus. When **we** are suffering as **He** suffered then we know the wonderful blessing of a deeper fellowship with Him.

The key to being faithful in suffering is being free from fear. We can only be free from **worldly** fear if we are full of **godly** fear. Peter reminds us of Isaiah 8:12–15. The world has all kinds of fears, both real and imagined. If we fall into **that** kind of fear we can be no help to them at all. Rather, we know that Jesus Christ is the LORD Almighty, the Rock that causes men to stumble, fall and be broken. All the fears in the world are nothing compared to falling into the hands of the Living God. As we fear Christ our LORD and Judge, so we are delivered from all other fears and are able to be of real use to our pagan friends in their fears. They will want to know why we do not fear what they fear – job loss, loneliness, illness, poverty, death, rejection or tragedy. Free from worldly fear we are prepared to give a proper explanation (verse 15) of the gospel **hope**. It is our hope of the future, our certainty about Jesus' return with His New Creation that enables us to cope with the loss of all things in this life.

However, our explanations must be given with 'gentleness and respect', verse 15. We might be tempted to humiliate unbelievers with carefully crafted human arguments, but this is not the gospel way – verse 16. It is vital that we do not undermine Jesus Christ through our ungodly behaviour. Rather, people should be ashamed of speaking against us because our behaviour is so good.

---

[1] (*continued*) 21:1-9 & 1 Samuel 22:6-23, but David wrote a different Psalm about all that – Psalm 52.

3. Christ's Example (3:17–22)

If we suffer for doing evil we cannot claim to be following the will of God. Jesus Christ Himself is the ultimate example of suffering evil for doing good. In accordance with God's will, as an innocent and righteous man (verse 18), Jesus suffered for everybody's sins to bring us to God. Jesus is such a good encouragement to us, because when we look at Him we see how He was ultimately vindicated by His Father. Yes, His body was killed on the Cross, but on the third day His body was resurrected by the Holy Spirit. The Holy Spirit also allowed Him to go and proclaim this victory to the spirits who had been disobedient during the life of Noah.

It might seem very strange for Peter to take us back to the life of Noah here. Noah was also a man who suffered for doing good. Nearly the whole world rejected his preaching (see 2 Peter 2:5), and only 8 people took advantage of the safety of the ark through Noah's faithful warnings. How ridiculous Noah must have seemed to the world of his day, building a boat for a worldwide Flood! Nevertheless, Noah was faithful to the Living God and he was saved when the time of judgement came. **He** was vindicated and the world was destroyed.

So, why did Jesus, through the Spirit, preach to the spirits who disobeyed in Noah's day? There have been several views on the subject:

- Jesus gave all the people who died through the Flood a second chance to believe in Him. This seems very unlikely because it goes against verses like Hebrews 9:27.
- Jesus was preaching to the world **through** Noah when Noah was preaching about the Flood long ago.
- After His Resurrection, Jesus, in the Spirit, went to declare His victory to the angels (the sons of God of Genesis 6:1–6[2]) who disobeyed God before the Flood by having relationships with human women.[3] In this way, Noah was vindicated **even** to those evil spirits.

Whatever is the right view, the conclusion is clear. Noah suffered for gospel faithfulness, but Christ vindicated him. Christ Himself suffered for doing good, yet He was also vindicated. So, we too must be encouraged to suffer for doing good, with the total confidence that these examples give us.

---

[2] In Job 1:6 the angels are also called 'the sons of God'.

[3] This explains the giant children they produced. Jude 6-7 seems to also refer to this ancient angelic immorality. See also 2 Peter 2:4-5 for more about angelic sin during the days of Noah. Genesis 6:4 could be Moses explaining how all the ancient myths began about great heroes being the offspring of gods and women. Moses lets us know that it was not 'a golden age' but a very wicked age.

This is why Noah's ark is a symbol of baptism. Anyone who wanted to survive the flood waters of judgement had to join with the people of God in the only place of safety, the Ark. In baptism a person is marked out as a member of the Body of Jesus Christ, the only place of safety on the day of God's judgement. Notice that Peter insists that the power of baptism is not in the water on our bodies, but in the resurrection of Jesus.

In verse 22, Peter again shows us Christ's total vindication over the whole creation from bottom (the spirits in prison) to top (heaven at the Father's right hand). Not just the good angels, but even the authorities and powers (see Ephesians 6:12) are in submission to the resurrected and ascended Jesus.

4. The End of all Things is Near (4:1–7a)

If we want to share that kind of final vindication, then we must embrace Jesus Christ in our hearts and minds. His attitude to life, to suffering and the future, must be our own attitude if we are to be authentic followers.

Peter singles out our attitude to sin as the test of our faith in Christ. Christ did not cling onto His body, but gave it up willingly on the Cross. If we take that same view of our bodies then we will not indulge all our so-called 'bodily instincts' but leave behind our evil desires. Our current, decaying bodies must all perish, so we cling to the will of our Father God, where the real future lies.

We have all spent far too much time wasting our lives in evil desires, 4:3. We might feel that we haven't given ourselves very much to these evil desires, but Peter warns us that any time at all in such evil desires is too much time. The kind of hedonistic lifestyle he describes is built on the assumption that this earthly life is all that there is, that there will be no Judgement Day and no Resurrection. To the world, verse 4, it seems very strange that we would avoid sexual immorality, drunkenness, wild parties and wanting lots of money (Ephesians 5:5). Surely those are the very things worth having in life! No, they are worthless, hateful, soul-destroying death traps when viewed from the perspective of the future in Jesus Christ. 1 Peter 4:5 gives us the stark truth that changes everything. Every person must stand before Jesus Christ, the Almighty God, to answer for their lives.

Whether we are living or dead, when that day comes the whole human race will be judged by Him. So, verse 6, **since the world began**, the gospel has been preached as **the** choice of life and death. Therefore, the same judgement will fall upon everybody, even those who died thousands of years ago.

Verse 6: humanity may pass one kind of judgement on us in terms of our bodily life, by rejecting us, ridiculing us or even killing us as happened to Jesus Himself. Nevertheless, a very different judgement needs to control our lives, the judgement of God. Our bodies suffer and die, but by the Spirit we may live the eternal life of God right now as we are faithful to Jesus Christ.

The slogan that must control our thinking and living from morning to night is this: **the end of all things is near**.

Further Questions ...

1. Why does Peter say 'whoever has suffered in the flesh is done with sin', 4:1? What does this mean? Romans 5:3–5; 6:5–6; Galatians 5:24; Hebrews 2:10.

2. 1 Peter 3:15 tells us to be ready to give the reason for our gospel hope. What does this mean? In history it was sometimes taken to mean that we should develop a system of philosophy to demonstrate the truth of the gospel. Often this ended up as little more than an argument for the existence of 'a god' and the historical truth of the Bible. Peter seems to have the Christian hope specifically in mind. What is the reason for our hope? How can we be ready to explain that? How did Jesus and His apostles give a reason for their hope?

Daily Readings ...

Day 1:   1 Peter 3:8–4:7

Day 2:   Psalm 34

Day 3:   1 Samuel 17:1–51, 21:10–15

Day 4:   Isaiah 8:11–9:7

Day 5:   Genesis chapter 6

Day 6:   Romans chapter 6

Day 7:   Titus chapter 3

BIBLE STUDY 4

1 Peter 3:8–18

1. Why is it so important to love our **Christian** brothers and sisters?

2. We often wonder what the will of God is for our lives, or about our 'calling' in life. What can we be sure it is, according to verse 9? How can we live out **this** calling practically this week? (verses 10–11)

3. Why, in verse 10, is there so much focus on what comes out of the mouth? See Matthew 12:34–36. How should we use our mouths instead, verse 15?

4. Looking at the quotation from Psalm 34, what is the 'blessing' mentioned in verse 9 that we receive? (Look especially at verse 12).

5. How is verse 12 a motivation for evangelism?

6. What is it that non-Christians fear? (Verse 14) How should we be different, according to Peter's quotation from Isaiah 8? (Look especially at verses 12–13 of the Isaiah passage)

7. Verse 15. Are we prepared right now to be able to explain the gospel to someone? Take a few minutes to discuss or write down a simple explanation of the Cross.

8. What does Peter think we might be tempted to do when talking about our hope in verse 15? How will doing the opposite of this aid our ministry, verse 16?

9. Why does Peter say it is better to suffer for doing good than evil, verse 18? What is the will of God on this subject (see also 2:15; 4:19)? Think about how this might change our prayers. Should we always pray that our persecution be taken away… or is there a different way to pray?

STUDY 5 - 1 PETER 4:7b-19

Sharing In Sufferings - And Glory

Key Truth: We rejoice through our trials, knowing that we identify with Jesus in His suffering.

1. Faithfully Administering God's Grace (4:7-11)

Peter has just reminded us in 4:6 that the Old Testament saints had the gospel preached to them and during their lives they suffered with their eyes fixed on the Messiah, living in the Spirit. The Messiah came as promised and fulfilled the things they looked forward to. Having read about these things, we have even more of a motivation to live in the way Peter describes.

The end is near, verse 7. That is, we are not just thinking about our own deaths (or the death of the Old Testament believers in verse 6) but it is the end of **everything** which is near. The gospel prepares us for thinking in this way, thinking on such a big and ultimate canvas. Living in the light of the end of everything is what sets us free to walk the path of rejection and suffering that Jesus has marked out for us. With our eyes fixed on the Resurrection future, we can endure being judged by men in the flesh, because we are living by the Spirit (as shown in 3:18) with Jesus as our pattern.

This is how we can pray with a clear mind and live a life of self-control. If we fix our vision on the 'here and now' then our prayers decay into shopping lists for earthly blessings and we tend to see self-denial as pointless and impossible. If we keep the **end** in mind we can pray for eternal, gospel matters and see through the worthless corruption of our evil desires.

Jesus Christ is coming back. So, above all else we must love one another fervently, verse 8. As the unbelieving world will constantly reject us and cause us to suffer, we must look after each other as Christians. We share our resources with other believers because we share the same goal.

Verse 8 talks of the love of 1 Corinthians 13, keeping no record of wrongs and thinking no evil of each other. We must be quick to forget and let go when people offend us. In Peter's mind, it's not worth taking offence at our brothers and sisters in the light of the end when Christ will be revealed.

But, Peter knows that we are difficult and sinful people, so he refers us to Proverbs, the practical manual on Christian living. Proverbs chapter 10 focuses on using our gifts for the uplifting of the Church, a guide to speaking and acting wisely. This is love in action. Proverbs describes life lived in harmony with the Divine Person called Wisdom, the One who makes us right with God, the Messiah.[1]

The Greek word used in verse 10 for 'whatever' gifts means literally 'multicoloured' gifts. It is the same word used about trials in 1:6. The grace of God matches the depth and variety of challenges, suffering and pain that the Church must face. We can stand through everything if we stand **together** with all the gifts God has given.

All charismatic gifts can be summarized as either **speaking** or **serving** gifts, verse 11. These are gifts that God has given to us to support the rest of the Church. So if we have the charismatic gift of speaking, everything we say must be **scripture only** – 'the very words of God'. Our own ideas won't sustain anyone, certainly not through times of suffering. Another example Peter mentions is the gift of hospitality. Sometimes we don't want to open our homes and share our lives with people, especially if it requires extra effort on our part. However, we do it self-consciously to serve the rest of the Church in God's ability.

Notice that in verse 11, God is only glorified **through** Jesus, when it is acknowledged or proclaimed that all the glory and all the dominion belong to Jesus Christ.

2. Don't be Surprised at Suffering (4:12)

The whole argument of the book of 1 Peter can be distilled to this very verse, verse 12 – don't be surprised at suffering.

The gospel of Mark records for us a very clear account of how Peter came to learn this vital truth about the Christian life, in a way he was not likely to forget. Look at Mark 8:31–36. Peter (like us all) wanted to run away from suffering, but when he gave in to such thinking he deeply offended Jesus. Imagine being called Satan by Jesus! What a way for Peter to learn that we must suffer as Christians and fix ourselves on a

---

[1] It is fascinating to make a list of all the qualities and benefits of the Person called Wisdom in the first 9 chapters.

glory that is to come. It is no wonder that he wants to tell us these things. He cares about this truth with passionate conviction.

Expecting a comfortable, trouble-free life, is not godly. It is worldly, and according to Jesus, it is inspired by the devil himself. If we expect a comfortable life, we will easily justify our silence and compromise with excuses such as: 'I don't want to offend people by talking about the gospel', or: 'I've got to be real to the people around me', or perhaps: 'we'll build bridges first and cross them later'. Christian history is littered with uncrossed bridges. The mentality that says 'I'll compromise now and be on fire for Jesus later' will never make the hard decisions that are needed. If we can't make them now, how will we make them then?

3. Rejoice That You Share in Christ's Suffering (4:13–14)

Peter tells us to 'rejoice (literally) **to the extent**' that we share in Christ's sufferings. Such a statement turns the world upside down. The more we suffer, the more we will rejoice! How can this make sense? How can we find the deepest joy in the deepest suffering?

When we are rejected, ridiculed, ignored or hurt for the name of Christ, **then** we experience our unity with Him most deeply. This union with Christ in suffering is so precious because it frees us to look forward to His return more eagerly. 1 Peter 1:6–7 laid this foundation at the beginning. It is the testimony of Christians of every age all over the world that their most joyful times have been the times when they have suffered most. They have found Jesus more real and faithful than they ever knew before.

Many manuscripts record an extra line to verse 14, as follows: 'On their part He is blasphemed, but on your part He is glorified' which explains the rest of the verse. When we are insulted because of Christ, our accusers think that they are injuring the Spirit in blasphemy. But actually they are identifying us with the Name of Jesus, giving us more of a reason to glorify God. Verse 16 shows again how it is that we glorify God during these times.

4. Judgement Begins With the Family of God (4:15–19)

There may be few murderers or thieves among us now as we study God's word together. However, how many of us have never busied ourselves in other peoples' affairs? We may be surprised to find 'meddler' listed amongst these other grave sins. Many Christians feel it is our duty to advise our unbelieving friends how to live their lives. Verse 15 tells us that meddling is not being Christian: it is being a moralizer, and has a place alongside other sins. Do we believe in justification by faith alone? Then that is what we must preach to unbelievers. What good will it do for the soul of a person who is denying the Living God to live a slightly more moral life? They still need the gospel message in order to please God. It is not our task to tell unbelievers to live their pagan lives in a more outwardly moral manner. Holy living **begins** when a person trusts in Jesus the Messiah.

We already know that we will suffer for being a Christian. We are warned here about revenge with a reminder of the terrible judgement that is to come for the wicked. If the LORD lets His own people whom He dearly loves suffer now, how much greater will the suffering be for those who deny Him? Again, Peter returns to the Scriptures to make his point really clear. Proverbs 11:31–12:1 talks of the benefit of discipline, and we already know from Proverbs 3:11–12 that discipline is actually a sign that God loves and cares for us. If you suffer as a Christian – praise God – because your suffering now is a chastisement that shows God loves you and that He wants you to be fruitful.

This brings us to verse 19 – when we suffer because we are Christians, we know **then** more than ever that we are in the very centre of God's will and therefore we can confidently commit ourselves to our Creator.

God our Creator: this title helps us picture the big cosmic view of the world. Our Father made the earth and each person on it – He is in ultimate control of us and also those that persecute us. We can lift our vision from our own little situation to our Father in heaven, seated on the throne of the whole universe. He is worthy of full commitment and trust. He has promised to make everything work for the good of the Church, and we can trust Him to do for us what He did for Jesus Himself.

Further Questions ...

1. What are the gifts mentioned in verse 10? Romans 12:3–8; 1 Corinthians 12, 14:12; Ephesians 4:7–13.

2. Why does Peter use the word 'judgement' when referring to the family of God in verse 17? See passages such as Proverbs 3:11–12; 1 Corinthians 4:1–4; Hebrews 4:11–13.

3. What does it mean that love 'covers over a multitude of sins', verse 8? Leviticus 19:11–18; Proverbs 17:9; James 5:20.

Daily Readings ...

Day 1:	1 Peter 4:7–19
Day 2:	1 Corinthians chapter 12
Day 3:	1 Corinthians chapter 13
Day 4:	1 Corinthians chapter 14
Day 5:	Mark 8:27–9:13
Day 6:	John chapter 15
Day 7:	Proverbs chapter 10

BIBLE STUDY 5

1 Peter 4:7-14

1. How do we keep a clear mind and exercise self-control? (Verse 7). What does Peter say will be the result of being clear minded and self controlled? Why?

2. How does love cover sins, verse 8?

3. What does Peter assume we are prone to doing when offering hospitality to each other (verse 9)? Is there anyone in our church family who would especially benefit from our hospitality? Who needs long term care and how can we support them together?

4. In verse 10, how do we each faithfully administer God's grace? There is a danger of focussing too much on what we might do on a Sunday at our church meeting. Think about how we can use our wide range of gifts in Christ's service through the whole week.

5. How does Peter show the big responsibility that is placed on those who preach and teach, verse 11? See also James 3:1. From where should they get their teachings? See 2 Timothy 3:16–17.

6. What does it mean to serve in the strength of the Living God? What practical difference does this make? (See 2 Corinthians 12:10)

7. How does Peter show what normal life is as a Christian, verse 12? Do we accept this? Can we think of examples in the Bible where persecuted Christians rejoice in the midst of their sufferings? What can we learn from them? Some examples are Acts 5:40–42 and Psalm 52.

Clothed With Humility – Firm in the Faith

Key Truth: Spiritual maturity is shown through submission and humility. Worldly prosperity and comfort is nothing compared with the glory which is to come.

1. Eager to Serve (5:1–4)

Peter begins the chapter by reminding us that he was an eye-witness of Christ's sufferings. In this we see Peter's wonderful humility. When we think about the way in which Peter saw Christ's sufferings we are thinking about a time when Peter **couldn't** face the prospect of suffering. We have already thought about his Satanic rejection of suffering in Mark 8, but we must also think of the way that Peter vehemently denied Jesus completely during His trial. Surely with such a disappointing record Peter was unsure of his standing with Jesus... but in 5:1 he goes on to say that he is 'one who also will share in the glory to be revealed'.

So many of Peter's readers down the centuries will have run away from suffering many times, but **Peter's own life shows us that we can begin again and walk the way of the crucified Jesus to the future glory**.

How many of us would claim to be an eye-witness of His suffering rather than an eye-witness of the miracles? How many of us prefer to talk of the **power** of Jesus rather than the **sufferings** of Jesus?

Peter goes on in verse 2 to refer to the elders as 'shepherds of God's flock'. Why does Peter choose this language? If we read John 21:15–19 we can see right away. After Peter had denied Jesus, Jesus went out of His way to carefully restore Peter by appointing him as a **shepherd** of His flock. The language of sheep and shepherds was obviously deep in Peter's heart and mind.

In John chapter 21 Jesus keeps the issue of suffering in front of Peter for his whole life. Peter knew he was going to die a horrible death for the sake of Jesus Christ. Jesus told him that he would glorify God through this suffering and death, just as Jesus had done. He knew that his life would end in martyrdom. When Peter spoke about the reality of suffering he was not speaking from an ivory tower.

The glory and joy of the servant of Jesus is in sharing the life and death of Jesus through all the suffering and rejection. That is why the model of leadership we have is so radically different to the world. In verse 3 Peter goes back to the teaching of Jesus in Matthew 20:25–8. The world (the Gentiles) exercise authority over people and lord it over people. The godly leader is a servant not a lord.

This caring service must not be grudging but whole-hearted and genuine. The leader cannot be an example of the teaching of Jesus unless they honestly believe it in their heart. The care of the elder comes by showing the glory and joy that comes through sacrificial service and suffering. Nobody can show this unless they love this truth in Jesus. It is Jesus alone who is our inspiration and guarantee (verse 4) as we wait for His appearing.

If Jesus can trust you to be faithful when He is your only comfort and joy, then you have embraced the way of Jesus. If you can say that you would be eager to **serve** in a situation where there is no power, no respect and no money then you have true spiritual maturity. But, if the LORD never calls me to any of those circumstances, it looks likely that He simply doesn't trust me to be a shepherd to His flock.[1]

What could sustain us in such a life? It is verse 4. Our reward is the crown of glory He is bringing for His fellow shepherds who have followed His pattern. Jesus will always thank us and encourage us even if nobody else ever does.

2. Humble Yourselves (5:5–7)

Verse 5 begins with younger **people** rather than specifically younger **males**, then moves on to 'all of you'. Younger people will always be tempted to assume that they know better than the older people. They will imagine that they have seen what older people have done wrong, that they can see through the 'compromise' and 'mediocrity' of the previous

---

[1] Isn't it strange that 'after much thought and prayer' many of us just happen to discover that the will of God for our lives involves comfort, security, affirmation and a regular income in an area that is socially advantaged? Many churches close down in 'difficult areas' simply because the LORD does not 'call' anyone to go there… or could it be that His call and way are not acceptable to us?

generation. Peter explains how the sacrificial way of Jesus applies to this. The young need to submit to the old.

But, arrogance is not the exclusive property of the young, so Peter goes on to include us all – all of you '**clothe** yourselves with humility towards one another.' Humility must cover us from head to foot. The quotation from Proverbs 3 shows us how it works. Proverbs 3 is a meditation on humility. The chapter is Solomon being instructed by his father David about Wisdom, the title given to the Messiah in the book of Proverbs. In verse 5 the young Solomon learned that he must not trust in his own understanding, but trust in the LORD with all his heart. In verse 7 he learned not to be wise in his own eyes. In verses 11–12 he learned that suffering is a sign that the LORD loves him. In verses 13–26 he learned that Wisdom is the key to the universe. All this is brought to the mighty conclusion that we are not to follow the wicked, however desirable their lifestyle or thinking. We do this simply because our eye is on the LORD, who befriends the humble but mocks the proud. We must always ask ourselves 'whose friendship do I want in life?' Whose friendship sustains me through life?

If we are clear on God's love of humility and hatred of pride, then (verse 6) we are ready to humble ourselves under the mighty hand of God. Under that mighty hand is the place we want to be, because though it opposes the proud its mightiness will be used to lift up the humble and use us for His mighty purposes. We can learn about 'God's mighty hand' in Exodus 3:19; 6:1 and Deuteronomy 9:26–9. We can confidently humble ourselves under a mighty hand that is capable of such wonderful redemption and judgement. This is why we can throw all our anxiety on Him. He cares for those who humble themselves under Him.

3. Be Self-Controlled and Alert (5:8–9)

Although we cast all our cares on our Heavenly Father, yet this is not an invitation to be careless. The devil is a very real danger. He is our **enemy**. Any difficulty we get from the unbelieving world comes from its service to the devil who opposes the way of Jesus Christ with uncompromising hatred. As long as we are simply religious, talking about 'god' in general, and keeping quiet about Jesus and the gospel, the devil will happily leave us alone. It is when we insist on publicly talking about Jesus that this powerful and cunning enemy will turn against us. When we genuinely walk the way of Jesus we are walking onto the spiritual battleground.

In the movies the devil is a chaotic, almost stupid individual who simply wants to create as much **immediate** suffering as he possibly can. However, according to Peter that is not the danger of the devil. The devil is much more interested in us living comfortable and easy lives.

If chapter 1:6–7 is true, then the Church **standing firm under suffering** is the last thing that the devil wants. He would much prefer us to live our lives in useless contentment, happy with good food, the respect of the people around us, sufficient money, a nice house in the country and the admiration of our work colleagues. The devil wants us to think that we can follow Jesus without the shame, suffering and rejection that He had to endure.

> **A Christian who has been devoured by the devil may have plenty of money, popularity, good health and comfort, but doesn't share the gospel with their friends, colleagues and neighbours**.

Therefore, verse 9, we resist the devil when we put Peter's letter into practice. We stand firm in the faith when we value the friendship of Jesus above all else. If He gives us comfort for a while we thank Him for it, but if He calls us to bear suffering, shame and loss then we are content with that as well as simply looking to Him to sustain us with His joy and love through it all.

The devil prowls around seeing whose life he can make easier, whose witness he can destroy through worldly comfort and worthless human honour.

It is so easy to use our children as an excuse for our own worldliness and compromise. If we will place 'the future of our children' (in terms of their education, home, money and worldly 'security') above their involvement in the mission of Jesus and the future of the world, then we will never unduly disturb the devil... and neither will our children. If they have learned from us to invest in the here and now, they are almost certain to live their lives just as we have taught them. How often when asked about our children do we respond with answers about their careers, educational success or sporting achievements rather than their faithfulness to the way of Jesus the Messiah?

Peter tells us to look around the world at the Christians who are standing firm in suffering. Has the devil devoured them? Do they know the strength and joy of Jesus? Has Jesus ever disappointed them?

4. The God of all Grace (5:10–11)

Just when it all seems to be too much for us, Peter has saved the best till last. Whatever suffering and rejection we may have to endure in the gospel work of Jesus, the Living God 'will **Himself** restore you and make you strong', verse 10. He has called us to His eternal glory in Jesus Christ, and He will never abandon us. After we have suffered 'a little while' He will make everything better at the end. Everything we have suffered will be paid back in full with massive rates of interest.

Peter's message is this: if you want **real** comfort and rest, then wait a little while and get better things than you ever dreamed of. How small all our sufferings will seem as we eat together on Resurrection Morning at the marriage-feast of Jesus!

The devil can offer us nothing more than comfort and ease for this short life. Jesus guarantees us **everlasting** glory with Him in the Renewed Creation with resurrection bodies. It doesn't take a genius to do the maths on this one!

5. Stand Fast in the Friendship of God (5:12–17)

Peter wrote this letter with the help of Silas. Mentioning Silas takes us back to Acts 16 when we see Paul and Silas enduring suffering in just the way Peter describes. In Philippi they were 'severely flogged' (Acts 16:23) for telling people about Jesus. In prison they continued to declare the gospel to anybody and everybody. Even after they were released they just moved on to Thessalonica to suffer the same kind of treatment. The ministry of Silas is an example of a Christian who loved Jesus more than a comfortable, quiet life.

So, with Silas' help, Peter has written this brief letter to testify to the fact that what he has said is the **true** grace of God, the genuine friendship of the Living God. There is no other way.

Verse 13 might sound odd at first, but in the Bible, Babylon is a symbol of the world in rebellion against God – see Revelation 18. The woman who sends her greetings seems to be the Church, the Bride of Jesus, from around the world encouraging us to stand fast in the gospel.

Mark also sends his greetings. The gospel of Mark is the gospel that focuses on **suffering** as the true glory of Jesus.

The letter concludes in such a touching way. We are gathered together as a persecuted minority sheltering under the mighty hand of God. The world under the power of the devil is set against us. Nevertheless, we love each other with sincerity. As the friends of God we don't give ourselves any more difficulties. Peace is the inheritance of all who live in Jesus Christ.

Further Questions ...

1. What is the result of being devoured by Satan, verse 8? See passages such as 1 Chronicles 21:1–3 and 13–14; Zechariah 3:1; Mark 8:31–36; 2 Corinthians 2:10–11; 2 Timothy 2:25–26.

2. So many of the compromises and sins of the Christian life go back to the fact that we do not give ourselves 100% to Jesus. He is no longer the beginning and end of our lives day-by-day. Perhaps we try to find ultimate intimacy with others, even if that takes us into sinful relationships. We want security in terms of **this** world and **this** age. We want the kind of peace that the world gives rather than the peace that Jesus gives. Think about how our hearts and minds stray away from warm devotion and dependence on Jesus, the Father and the Holy Spirit? What role does daily Bible reading play in all this? How much time do we talk to our heavenly Father each day in comparison to other people? What priority does the Living God have in our daily schedules?

3. Why is it an encouragement to know that our brothers throughout the world are undergoing the same kind of sufferings as us, verse 9? See 1 Corinthians 12:25–26; 2 Corinthians 1:3–11. How can we show solidarity with the suffering Church around the world? Pick a nation in which the Church is being overtly persecuted and find out about the churches and the Christians involved. Who has been arrested and who has been killed? How do the churches keep meeting? What are the main prayer requests? Can we write to anybody to express support or can we appeal to their government to cease the persecution? We will find that our own faithfulness and courage will be greatly strengthened as we learn about the faithful witness of other Christians.

Daily Readings ...

Day 1:   1 Peter chapter 5

Day 2:   Ezekiel chapter 34

Day 3:   John 9:35–10:21.

Day 4:   Philippians 2:1–17

Day 5:   Proverbs chapter 3

Day 6:   2 Corinthians chapter 1

Day 7:   John chapter 21

BIBLE STUDY 6

1 Peter Chapter 5

1. What does it mean to be humble (verse 6)? What will sustain our humility each day?

2. Why do we humble ourselves under 'the mighty hand of God' (verse 6)? What does the Bible teach us about His mighty hand and how does this help us to be humble before Him? (Exodus 3:19 and Deuteronomy 9:26–9)

3. What does verse 7 have to say about the very special relationship a Christian has with God the Father?

4. According to Peter, how does Satan attack our faith? (Look at Mark 8:31–33). How then can we resist him?

5. Are we making sure that we are encouraging our brothers and sisters in the Lord in other parts of the world where they are suffering for the gospel more than we are, verse 9? In what ways can we do this?

6. How can Peter describe his many years of suffering for Jesus as 'a little while' verse 10?

7. Think back on our studies from the book of 1 Peter. What main points have you learned? Try to share these with another Christian to encourage our walk with Christ.